Savvy

LOTIONS, POTIONS, and *Polish*

DIY CRAFTS AND RECIPES
for Hands, Nails, and Feet

by AUBRE
ANDRUS

CAPSTONE PRESS
a capstone imprint

Savvy Books are published by Capstone Press,
1710 Roe Crest Drive, North Mankato, Minnesota 56003
www.mycapstone.com

Library of Congress Cataloging-in-Publication Data
Names: Andrus, Aubre, author.
Title: Lotions, potions, and polish : DIY crafts and recipes for hands,
nails, and feet / by Aubre Andrus.
Description: North Mankato, Minnesota : Capstone Press, [2017] | Series:
Savvy. DIY Day Spa | Audience: Age 9-13. | Audience: Greade 4 to 6. |
Identifiers: LCCN 2016030041| ISBN 9781515734451 (library binding) |
ISBN 9781515734499 (eBook PDF)
Subjects: LCSH: Hand—Care and hygiene—Juvenile literature. | Nails
(Anatomy)—Care and hygiene—Juvenile literature. | Foot—Care and
hygiene—Juvenile literature. | Handicraft—Juvenile literature.
Classification: LCC RA777 .A53 2017 | DDC 646.7/27—dc23
LC record available at https://lccn.loc.gov/2016030041

Editor: Eliza Leahy
Designer: Tracy McCabe
Creative Director: Heather Kindseth
Production Specialist: Katy LaVigne

Image Credits: Photographs by Capstone Studio: Karon Dubke,
photographer; Sarah Schuette, photo stylist; Marcy Morin,
studio scheduler; Author photo by Ariel Andrus

Printed and bound in the USA.
010062S17

TABLE OF CONTENTS

INTRODUCTION

Creating a spa experience at home is easier than you might think. Believe it or not, you can find a lot of what you need in the kitchen. The recipes in this book aren't much different from traditional recipes (such as cupcakes, cookies, and cake), but these recipes aren't meant to be eaten. Instead of soothing your hunger, these recipes soothe your skin—specifically your hands and feet!

Everything from embarrassing foot odor to mistake-free nail art is covered in this book. Your hands and feet will be relieved of dry skin (thanks to scrubs and masks!) and muscle aches and pains (thanks to creams and soaks!). And, of course, they'll look great too. Looking beautiful is all about feeling beautiful!

Flip through these pages to find your favorite projects in the same way you'd flip through a cookbook. There's no wrong or right place to start. There's a homemade spa product for everyone, from lotions to sprays to soaks. We even added some essential oils to these recipes so your DIY spa experience is as relaxing as the real thing.

Enjoy these products alone, give them as gifts, or invite some friends over for a spa party.

IT'S TIME TO PAMPER YOURSELF!

SPECIALTY INGREDIENTS

Some of the recipes in this book call for simple ingredients that you may already have in your kitchen, such as baking soda, olive oil, or vanilla extract. But there are some specialty ingredients that you likely won't find at home.

Luckily, they can be found at health food stores or organic grocery stores near the spices, pharmacy, or beauty aisles. You can also find them online. Here are some of those ingredients and the reasons you need them in your recipes.

beeswax pastilles

shea butter

Epsom salts

Beeswax – Beeswax helps firm balms and creams. These recipes call for grated beeswax, which can be made by using a cheese grater on a bar of pure beeswax. If you'd rather not grate your beeswax, you could buy beeswax pastilles, which are small granules or pellets.

Coconut Oil – Coconut oil moisturizes your skin and hair.

Distilled Water – Distilled water has been boiled to remove impurities, and it will help your ingredients last longer. It can be found at grocery stores.

Epsom Salts – Epsom salts soothe aching muscles and relieve itching from dry skin and insect bites.

Jojoba Oil – Jojoba oil is soothing when applied to skin and can help calm the effects of acne and sunburn.

Sea Salt – The rough texture of sea salt helps exfoliate skin while naturally detoxifying.

Shea Butter – Shea butter moisturizes, soothes, and balances skin without clogging pores. It can even help heal cuts and scrapes.

sea salt

ESSENTIAL OILS

Many of the recipes in this book call for essential oils. Essential oils are used for aromatherapy (they smell lovely and can make you feel great) and for health benefits for your hair, skin, and body.

They can be found at health food stores, organic grocery stores, or online. Here are the essential oils used in this book and the reasons you might use them in your recipes.

Lavender

Lavender is probably the most popular essential oil. It can soothe skin and possibly help fight acne. It has a calming floral aroma that can help you fall asleep.

Lemon*

Lemon essential oil is antibacterial. It can prevent infection when applied to the skin. Its citrus aroma is energizing.

Orange*

Orange essential oil is a natural cleanser and deodorizer, and it can help heal skin. Like lemon, its citrus aroma is energizing.

Peppermint

Peppermint essential oil has a cooling effect. It can relieve muscle pain and has an invigorating aroma that can make you feel alert.

Tea Tree

Tea tree oil fights bacteria, fungi, and viruses, so it can help treat athlete's foot, acne, and more when applied to the skin.

Orange   Lavender   Lemon   Peppermint   Tea Tree

Be careful! Don't allow any undiluted essential oil to get on your skin or in your eyes or mouth. Recipes from this book containing essential oils should not be used on children under age 6, and for older children, an adult's help is recommended.

*Lemon and orange essential oils could be phototoxic, which means they can make your skin extra-sensitive to the sun. Don't apply citrus essential oils to bare skin before going outside. And always wear sunscreen!

MEASURING YOUR INGREDIENTS

Essential oils are very potent and must be diluted with distilled water or a carrier oil, such as coconut oil, jojoba oil, or olive oil. It might not seem like you're using a lot, but a little goes a long way!

The recipes in this book dilute the essential oil to about 1 percent. That means some recipes require only a few drops. We measure essential oils by the drop in this book because it's hard to measure any other way. (There are 20 drops in 1 milliliter, and ¼ teaspoon is a little more than 1 milliliter.) There are very few recipes that will require more than ¼ teaspoon of essential oil.

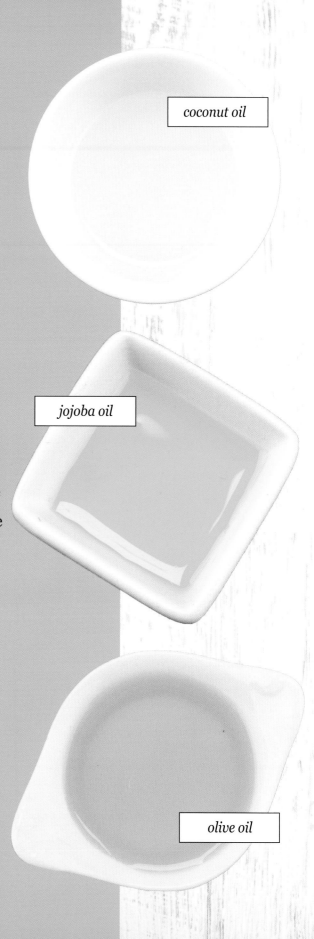

coconut oil

jojoba oil

olive oil

HOW TO SAFELY MELT BUTTER AND OIL

Shea butter is a soft solid that must be melted for many recipes in this book. A double boiler is best for melting oils and butters, but you can also microwave them at 50 percent power in 30-second increments, stirring in between, until the solid is almost all the way melted. Stir to complete the melting process. You don't want to overheat the oils or butters.

Coconut oil is also used in this book. Whether your coconut oil is a solid or a liquid depends on where you live, what time of year it is, and the air temperature. To solidify it, place it in the refrigerator until it hardens. To liquefy it, heat it in a microwave-safe bowl in 10-second increments at 50 percent power, stirring in between, until the solid is almost all the way melted.

It's best to heat the solids in a microwave-safe bowl with a pourable spout and a handle, such as a glass Pyrex measuring cup. Be sure to always wear an oven mitt when removing a hot bowl from the microwave.

HOW TO SAFELY STORE YOUR PRODUCTS

It's best to use glass containers, not plastic, to store any recipe that contains essential oils, because the essential oils can deteriorate plastic over time. All of the recipes in this book make small batches since they are natural and don't contain preservatives.

Unless indicated otherwise, the finished products should be stored in a cool, dry place and should be used within two to four weeks. Never use a recipe if it looks like it has grown mold, if it has changed colors, or if it begins to smell bad.

ALLERGIES

Some people have skin sensitivities and allergies. Check with your doctor or dermatologist before using any of these recipes.

CLEAN UP

Many of the recipes in this book use oils and butters, which might feel greasy. To clean up, wipe your hands and any used dishes with a dry paper towel first, then use soap and water to wash. When using recipes in the bathtub, such as sugar scrubs, wipe the floor clean with a dry towel afterward. Oils and butters can make surfaces slippery and unsafe.

WHERE TO FIND PACKAGING FOR YOUR PRODUCTS

It's important to use brand new containers to store your products. It will help prevent mold from growing. Here's where you can buy containers that are perfect for the recipes in this book:

• reusable 2-ounce (59-milliliter) glass bottles or 4-ounce (118-mL) glass containers can be found in the essential oil aisle at health food stores

• reusable 2-ounce (59-mL) plastic spray bottles or 3-ounce (89-mL) plastic squeeze bottles can be found in the travel section of grocery or convenience stores

• reusable 4-ounce (118-mL) spice tins or empty spice jars can be found in the bulk spice aisle in grocery stores or health food stores

• half-pint glass jars can be found in the jam or canning aisle in grocery stores or health food stores

• round plastic containers with screw-top lids can be found in the jewelry or bead storage aisle at craft stores or in the travel aisle of department stores

Chocolate Sugar Hand Scrub

You will need:

- ½ cup (120 mL) raw sugar
- ½ cup (120 mL) packed brown sugar
- 1 tsp (5 mL) baking cocoa
- 3 tbsp (45 mL) olive oil
- ½ tsp (2.5 mL) vanilla extract

This scrub smells good enough to eat—and technically, you could! It turns out that sugar is great for polishing your hands. To use, spoon a scoop into your hands and rub hands together gently over a sink. Rinse, then pat hands dry with a clean towel.

DIRECTIONS:

Mix all ingredients in a bowl. Scoop into a lidded glass container. Makes about 1 cup (240 mL). Store in a cool, dry place. Use within 3-4 weeks.

Cuticle Balms

No more dry cuticles! Give your nails extra attention and help prevent hangnails with these soothing balms. One recipe makes enough to fill several small containers, so you can give these away as gifts too! To use, massage on and around your nails three times per week.

Strengthening Lavender Balm

Moisturize and soften your cuticles, or the skin around your nails, and strengthen the nail itself with this lovely smelling balm.

beeswax pastilles

You will need:

6 tsp (30 mL) shea butter
3 tsp (15 mL) grated beeswax
   or beeswax pastilles
3 tsp (15 mL) jojoba oil
3 drops lavender essential oil

Whitening Lemon Balm

This cuticle balm goes a step further and can help whiten stained or yellowing nails, thanks to the lemon essential oil.

You will need:

6 tsp (30 mL) shea butter
3 tsp (15 mL) grated beeswax
   or beeswax pastilles
3 tsp (15 mL) jojoba oil
3 drops lemon essential oil

DIRECTIONS:

Scoop shea butter and beeswax into a microwave-safe bowl with a pourable spout. Microwave in 30-second increments at 50 percent power, stirring each time, until mixture mostly liquefies. Remove bowl with an oven mitt, and stir until mixture is clear, not cloudy. Add jojoba oil and stir. Let cool slightly, then add essential oil.

Carefully pour into small lidded containers. Let harden at room temperature. Makes enough to fill about six small circular containers. Store in a cool, dry place. Use within 3-4 weeks.

Hand Creams

Here's a moisturizing cream that will turn dry hands soft and shimmering—and it smells good too. To use, scoop a small amount into your palm. Massage hands together, working the lotion from your fingertips to your wrists. If your hands feel too oily, wipe them off with a dry paper towel.

Cooling Peppermint Hand Cream

This balm softens your skin and leaves it feeling cool—and don't forget about that invigorating minty scent!

jojoba oil

You will need:

¼ cup (60 mL) shea butter
1 tbsp (15 mL) beeswax or
   beeswax pastilles
⅛ cup (30 mL) jojoba oil
6 drops peppermint essential oil

Lavender Cream for Dry Hands

Lavender has a moisturizing effect on even the driest skin, but that's not all. Its floral scent is known to be curiously calming.

You will need:

¼ cup (60 mL) shea butter
1 tbsp (15 mL) beeswax or
   beeswax pastilles
⅛ (30 mL) cup jojoba oil
6 drops lavender essential oil

DIRECTIONS:

Scoop shea butter and beeswax into a microwave-safe bowl with a pourable spout. Microwave in 30-second increments at 50 percent power, stirring each time, until mixture mostly liquefies. Remove bowl with an oven mitt, and stir until clear, not cloudy. Add jojoba oil and stir. Let cool slightly, then add essential oil.

Carefully pour mixture into lidded glass jar. Let solidify at room temperature overnight. Makes about ½ cup (120 mL). Store in a cool, dry place. Use within 3-4 weeks.

Nail-Strengthening Serum

You will need:

4 tbsp (60 mL) jojoba oil
2 tbsp (30 mL) olive oil
10 drops lavender essential oil
5 drops lemon essential oil

There's nothing better for dry nails than jojoba oil. To use, add one drop to each nail, then massage onto the nail, under the nail, and around the cuticle. Apply this serum three days in a row or until your nails feel moisturized and strong.

olive oil

DIRECTIONS:

Mix all ingredients together in a bowl with a pourable spout. Pour into a glass bottle that has a dropper. Makes enough to fill a 3-ounce (89-mL) bottle. Store in a cool, dry place. Use within 3-4 weeks.

Warming Wrap

You will need:

¼ cup (60 mL) oats
¼ tsp (1.2 mL) ground cinnamon
¼ tsp (1.2 mL) cayenne pepper
1 tbsp (15 mL) honey
1 tbsp (15 mL) olive oil
1-2 tbsp (15-30 mL) warm distilled water
3 drops orange essential oil (optional)
2 washcloths

Slather this naturally warming paste onto your feet or your hands. Finish by wrapping each hand or foot with a warm washcloth. (Run warm water over a washcloth, then wring out the excess water.) Ask a friend to help with the last step. Leave on for 10 minutes, then rinse hands or feet in a bowl of water and pat dry with a clean towel.

DIRECTIONS:

Mix oats in a blender. Pour into a bowl, then stir in cinnamon, cayenne pepper, honey, olive oil, and essential oil. Stir in water until mixture reaches desired consistency. Makes enough paste for a mask for your hands or feet.

Sea Salt Hand Scrubs

This scrub is perfect for chapped winter hands. The coarse sea salt helps scrub off dead skin cells, and the olive oil will leave your skin feeling silky smooth. To use, spoon a small amount into palms. Rub hands together over the sink, working the mixture into your skin. Rinse, then pat hands dry with a clean towel.

Energizing Citrus Scrub

This citrus scrub smells bright, sweet, and squeaky clean!

You will need:

1 cup (240 mL) sea salt
½ cup (120 mL) olive oil
15-20 drops lemon or
orange essential oil

sea salt

Anti-Bacterial Hand Scrub

The tea tree essential oil in this recipe can help kill bacteria and fungus as well as alleviate itchiness.

You will need:

1 cup (240 mL) sea salt
½ cup (120 mL) olive oil
15-20 drops tea tree essential oil

DIRECTIONS:

Mix all ingredients in a bowl. Scoop into a lidded glass container. Makes about 1 cup (240 mL). Stir before each use. Store in a cool, dry place. Use within 3-4 weeks.

Press-On Nail Wraps

You will need:

plastic sandwich bag
colored nail polish
clear nail polish
permanent marker
toothpick (optional)

These nail wraps are simple to make but can add a lot of flair to your nails! Experiment with colors and designs until you find a combination you love.

DIRECTIONS:

Open a sandwich bag and slide your hand inside. Using a permanent marker, outline the shape of each of your nails. Flip the bag over. Following the nail stencil, paint nail polish within the lines. Make sure it's a thick enough layer that you will be able to peel it off in the future. You might need multiple coats of polish.

Let the nail polish dry, then top it with a design. A toothpick is helpful when making small details, like polka dots. Place a small dot of nail polish on the bag, then use your toothpick like a brush. Let dry overnight.

Carefully peel each wrap from bag. To use, paint your nails with a clear coat of nail polish first, then press on the decal while clear coat is still wet. If any excess decal hangs over the edge of your nail, trim with small manicure scissors or file away excess decal once the clear nail polish is dry.

Foot Soaks for Tired Toes

Give your feet a break! To use, fill a large bowl (big enough to fit both your feet) halfway with warm water. Pour ¾ cup (180 mL) of the mix into the bowl. Let your feet soak for 10-15 minutes, then pat dry with a clean towel. Discard the remaining liquid in the sink.

Re-energizing Mix

Bring your feet back to life after a long day. The peppermint in this soak will put some pep in your step!

baking soda

Epsom salts

You will need:

1 cup (240 mL) baking soda
½ cup (120 mL) Epsom salts
10 drops peppermint essential oil

Soothing Soak

Sensitive skin? This soak will calm and repair, as well as relax your mind, thanks to the spa-like scent of lavender.

You will need:

1 cup (240 mL) powdered milk
½ cup (120 mL) Epsom salts
5 drops lavender essential oil
   (optional)
3 drops orange essential oil
   (optional)

DIRECTIONS:

Mix all ingredients in a bowl, then pour into a lidded glass container until ready to use. Each recipe makes 1½ cups (360 mL), or enough for two foot soaks.

Gingerbread Foot Scrub

You will need:

- ½ cup (120 mL) white sugar
- ½ cup (120 mL) packed brown sugar
- 3 tbsp (45 mL) olive oil
- ½ tsp (2.5 mL) ginger
- ¼ tsp (1.2 mL) ground cinnamon
- ¼ tsp (1.2 mL) allspice
- ¼ tsp (1.2 mL) nutmeg
- ½ tsp (2.5 mL) vanilla extract

This mix won't make a batch of cookies, but it will make another sweet treat—for your feet! This scrub can also make a great gift when packaged in a pretty glass container.

To use, massage a scoop onto your feet while sitting over a bathtub or a large bowl of water. Rinse, then pat feet dry with a clean towel.

ginger

Be careful! Oils and butters can make bathtub surfaces slippery. A non-slip bath mat may help. Wipe bathtub floor with a dry towel when finished.

DIRECTIONS:

Mix all ingredients in a small bowl. Scoop into a lidded glass container. Makes about 1 cup (240 mL). Store in a cool, dry place, and use within 3-4 weeks.

Cooling Sore Muscle Butter

You will need:

- ½ cup (120 mL) coconut oil
- ½ cup (120 mL) shea butter
- 10 drops peppermint essential oil
- 15 drops tea tree essential oil

Pamper sore feet and tired toes. This butter melts as you massage it into your skin. Thanks to the peppermint and tea tree essential oils, it has a nice cooling effect. To use, massage a small scoop onto feet and lower legs.

shea butter

DIRECTIONS:

Scoop coconut oil and shea butter into a microwave-safe mixing bowl. Microwave in 30-second increments at 50 percent power, stirring each time, until mixture mostly liquefies. Remove bowl with an oven mitt, and stir until clear, not cloudy.

To turn the mixture into cream, cover bowl with plastic wrap and let cool in refrigerator until the texture resembles softened butter (this step should take no longer than an hour). If mixture fully hardens, remove from refrigerator and let it warm on the counter. Add essential oil, then whip with a hand mixer on low speed for 3-5 minutes, or until the color brightens and peaks form in the mixture.

When desired consistency is reached, scoop into jar with spatula. Makes about 1 cup (240 mL). Store in a cool, dry place. Use within 3-4 weeks.

Foot Repair Stick

You will need:

⅓ cup (80 mL) coconut oil
⅓ cup (80 mL) grated beeswax
   or beeswax pastilles
3 tbsp (45 mL) shea butter
16 drops tea tree essential oil
   (optional)
empty deodorant tube

Give your feet a break! Roll this soothing balm onto your feet before bed, focusing on dry, cracked heels. Rub in the excess balm with your fingers, then slip into a warm pair of socks. When your feet hit the floor in the morning, they'll be soft and smooth!

coconut oil

beeswax pastilles

Be careful! Don't pour any remaining mixture down the drain—it could cause a clog. Instead, let it harden overnight, then scoop it into a garbage bin.

DIRECTIONS:

Scoop shea butter and beeswax into a microwave-safe bowl with a pourable spout. Microwave in 30-second increments at 50 percent power, stirring each time, until mixture mostly liquefies. Remove bowl from microwave with an oven mitt. Stir in coconut oil until clear, not cloudy. Let cool slightly, then add essential oil.

Create a tight seal at the bottom of an empty deodorant tube by screwing canister to its lowest setting. (Reuse a deodorant tube or buy an empty deodorant tube at an online specialty shop.) Over a garbage can, carefully pour liquid into empty deodorant tube until full. Place cap on top and keep in refrigerator overnight until liquid solidifies.

Makes enough to fill an empty deodorant tube. Store in a cool, dry place. Use within 3-4 weeks.

Fresh Feet Spray

You will need:

- 4 tbsp (60 mL) apple cider vinegar
- 2 tbsp (30 mL) distilled water
- 6 drops tea tree essential oil

Smelly feet can be embarrassing, but this spray will help! Apple cider vinegar naturally absorbs smells and can help tame toenail fungus. Tea tree oil is known for deodorizing and healing too. Shake before each use.

apple cider vinegar

DIRECTIONS:

Mix all ingredients in a small bowl with a pourable spout. Pour into a 3-ounce (89-mL) spray bottle. Store in a cool, dry place. Use within 2 weeks.

Pedicure Slippers

After a pedicure, your nails need to dry before you can wear shoes. Make a pair of these foam slippers and you'll feel like you're at the salon. There's one difference: these slippers are a bit more glam! If you're having friends over for a pedicure party, make a few pairs in advance.

You will need:

12 x 18 inch (30 x 46 centimeter) piece of foam
scissors
pen
2 brads
3D flower stickers (optional)

DIRECTIONS:

Trace your feet or a pair of shoes onto a piece of foam. Now trace a second line ½ inch (1.2 cm) in from the outline of your feet. Cut along that outer line. On the inner line, draw a small X at the middle point of each side of foot. Puncture the foam with scissors at the left X and cut along the inner line and around the heel until you reach the right X.

Fold the recently cut end upward and secure with a brad at the top, near where you want your big toe to fit. The brad should puncture the foam easily. Makes 1 pair of slippers. Decorate with 3D flower stickers, glitter, rhinestones, or anything else you can think of to make your slippers stand out!

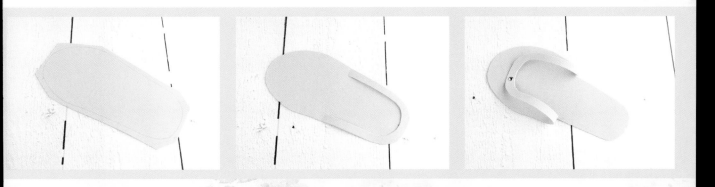

Tingly Salt Scrub for Feet

You will need:

- 1 cup (240 mL) sea salt
- ½ cup (120 mL) olive oil
- 12 drops peppermint essential oil
- 12 drops tea tree essential oil

After a good scrub, your feet will feel soft and smooth! The peppermint and tea tree essential oils cause a cooling, tingling effect during the process. To use, massage a handful onto your feet while sitting over a bathtub or a large bowl of water with a towel underneath it. Rinse, then pat feet dry with a clean towel.

sea salt

Be careful! Oils and butters can make bathtub surfaces slippery. A non-slip bath mat may help. Wipe bathtub floor with a dry towel when finished.

DIRECTIONS:

Mix all ingredients in a small bowl. Scoop into a lidded glass container. Makes about 1 cup (240 mL) or enough to fill a half-pint canning jar. Store in a cool, dry place. Use within 3-4 weeks.

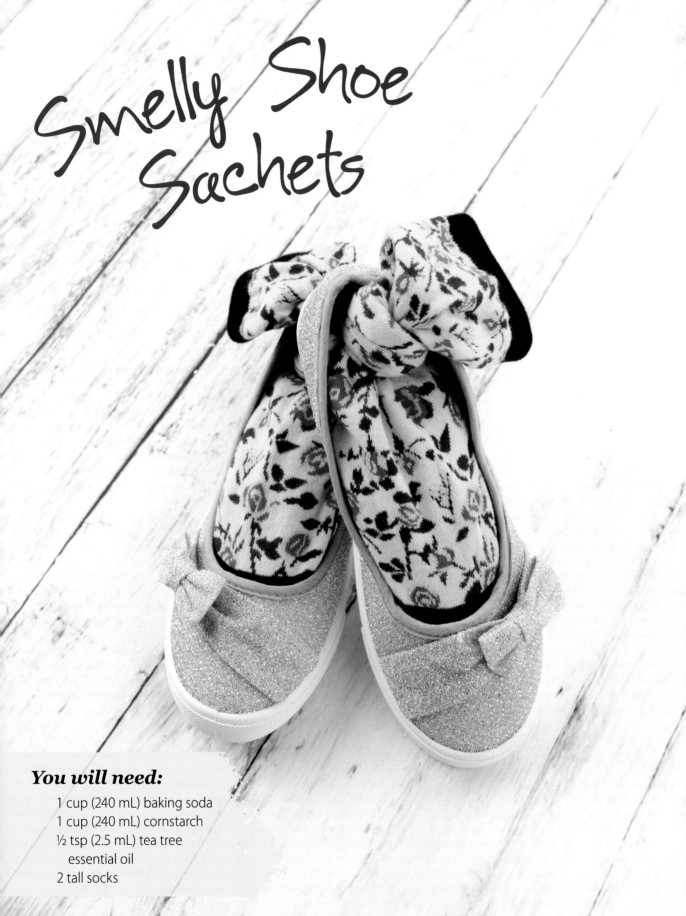

Smelly Shoe Sachets

You will need:

- 1 cup (240 mL) baking soda
- 1 cup (240 mL) cornstarch
- ½ tsp (2.5 mL) tea tree essential oil
- 2 tall socks

*The baking soda and tea tree
essential oil in this recipe will
help absorb the odor in your
favorite pair of shoes. To use,
place sachets snugly into the toe
of your shoe and let sit overnight
or for a few days. Replace the
ingredients every 3 months.*

baking soda

Tea Tree

cornstarch

DIRECTIONS:

Mix all ingredients together in a bowl with a pouring spout. Pour 1 cup
(240 mL) of mixture into each sock. (A funnel will help, and it's best to
place each sock in a bowl to catch the mess.) Tie remaining length of
sock tightly in a knot. Makes 2 sachets.

CONGRATS TO YOU!

You've made all-natural recipes that beautify your mind and body. Which one was your favorite? The calming or the rejuvenating? The scrubbing or the soothing?

It's important to pamper yourself every week—if not every day. Taking even just five minutes to relax with one of your favorite recipes can relieve stress, calm your nerves, and help you find focus.

Once you've spoiled yourself, don't forget to share the love by giving away these beauty products as gifts. Or throw a party and pamper your guests with spa-like treatments.

It's all about feeling beautiful in the skin you're in. When you feel beautiful, you look beautiful!

READ MORE

Berne, Emma Carlson. *Nail Care Tips & Tricks*. Style Secrets. Minneapolis: Lerner Publications, 2016.

Bolte, Mari. *Spa Projects You Can Make and Share*. Sleepover Girls Crafts. North Mankato, Minn.: Capstone, 2015.

Waite, Sara and **Samantha Tremlin**. *Pretty Hands & Sweet Feet*. Lake Forest, Cali.: Walter Foster Publishing, 2016.

Titles in this set:

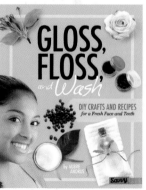

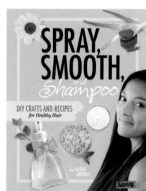

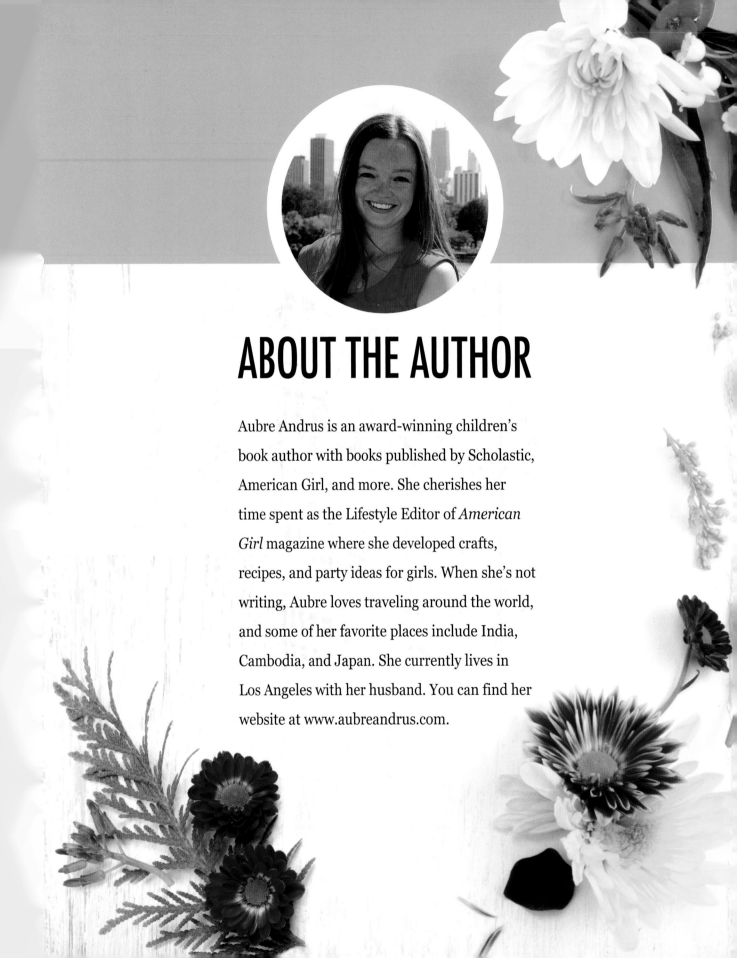

ABOUT THE AUTHOR

Aubre Andrus is an award-winning children's book author with books published by Scholastic, American Girl, and more. She cherishes her time spent as the Lifestyle Editor of *American Girl* magazine where she developed crafts, recipes, and party ideas for girls. When she's not writing, Aubre loves traveling around the world, and some of her favorite places include India, Cambodia, and Japan. She currently lives in Los Angeles with her husband. You can find her website at www.aubreandrus.com.